Silkworms / Bombyx M(

From Silkworm Egg(

How to make silk at home.

By

Elliott Lang

Published by IMB Publishing 2015

Table of Contents

Foreword

More than five millennia ago, the Chinese put an insect into the service of man, the silkworm or more appropriately *Bombyx mori*, the silk moth.

In its larval stage, this creature may be one of the hardest working insects in the world. Its existence is so intimately tied to luxury textile production that *Bombyx mori* can no longer exist independently in nature.

The adult moths have no working mouth parts. They come into the world for the purpose of mating. The males die shortly thereafter. The females lay their eggs, and then they also expire.

When the eggs hatch, a new generation of larva begins the four-stage molting process that culminates in the spinning of a cocoon.

This is not just any cocoon, however. It is made of one, long, continuous strand of pure white silk. When unwound, spun into thread, and woven, this cocoon becomes the most luxurious fabric known to man -- silk.

The opening of the fabled trade route dubbed the "Silk Road" brought this prized Oriental textile to the West, and in time, the Chinese lost their cherished monopoly in the process.

Silk is produced in many places around the world today. But the process is still dependent on silkworms, and largely on giving those worms a diet of white mulberry leaves.

Although there have been refinements in methodology in a mechanical sense, the whole industry is still based on well-fed worms spinning silken cocoons.

Raising silkworms can be undertaken in the home by enthusiastic "sericulturists." Most typically, when silkworms are raised at home it is for one of three reasons:

- To produce fiber that will be used by or sold to textile artisans.

- For the purpose of providing nutritionally rich food for reptiles and similar pets.

- Out of fascination with and appreciation for the worms as "pets" or as an instructional exercise for children.

Of these three endeavors, the one that raises the greatest potential to earn some "side money" from a home business is the production of pet food.

The most creative and arguably satisfying is the home production of silk fiber for personal use or for sale to artisans.

If you are considering entering the world of sericulture, the purpose of this book is to give you a complete overview of the process, and to explain the basics of raising silkworms.

I do look at the basics of harvesting silk from the cocoons, but I am of the opinion that if at all practical to do so, it is best to be mentored in this process by a skilled sericulturist.

You can connect with such individuals online, and often in traditionalist venues like renaissance fairs. By getting to know people who have been working with silkworms and silk for many years, you will pick up those little "tricks" of the trade that never seem to find their way into the written literature.

I had one sericulturist assure me that the best way to loosen silk fibers from a cocoon was with a toothbrush making straight motions while holding the cocoon in your hand. Another was a devotee of dish brushes used in a circular motion with the cocoons still in water.

You wouldn't think such a small choice would be of much consequence, but each person argued passionately – and at length – for their preferred method. Both sericulturists had developed a "process" that, while fundamentally the same, differed in fine points of execution they believed altered their finished product.

Understanding your options for extracting and spinning silk is crucial before you begin. To see various methods used, I recommend watching videos online. Videos will give you a real understanding of the process of unraveling or stretching silk.

I also recommend that you find someone to literally "hold your hand" the first time, that would be ideal. Seeking advice as you advance each step will be a tremendous help.

From the initial step, however, you may also find yourself wanting to learn how to spin silk thread, and then to dye the fiber. It's a short jump from those skills to becoming curious about weaving silk cloth.

My point is this, your initial idea may be to raise a few silkworms, but you have no idea where that will take you in the end! Covering all the possibilities from spinning to weaving is not the point of this text.

I hope to kindle your interest in sericulture. I hope you will come away from this book with an ability to ask the right questions and seek the right teachers to allow you to take your new hobby – or business – as far as you would like to go with it.

Regardless of your personal goals, this information will help you get started. By the time you reach the end of this book, you should have a firm grasp of the basics of acquiring eggs, husbanding them to hatch, and then caring for the worms until they spin their cocoons.

From there, I try to make you aware of your options for either profit or pleasure – or perhaps a bit of both.

Sericulture as a home endeavor is, frankly, what you choose to make of it.

Regardless, you are about to be introduced to an ancient technique that was largely responsible for opening up the lines of communication between the Eastern and Western Worlds more than 5 millennia ago.

In the process, the culture of both was irrevocably altered. The silkworms themselves, however, have simply continued to do what they were designed to do – create a completely natural fiber that is, for all practical purposes, "worm spit."

Chapter 1) – History of Silkworm Production

There are actually many different kinds of silkworms, but the one that has become the best domesticated insect in the world is *Bombyx mori*, the Mulberry Silkworm.

A) Types of Silkworms

There are more than 500 species of silkworms found in the wild. Only five, however, are commercially important in the making of marketable silk fiber.

Bombyx mori (also known as the Mulberry Silkworm) is the leader of this group, and the primary topic of this book. These silkworms produce the highest quality silk with the greatest diversity of uses. The fiber from their cocoons is typically unraveled in one, long, continuous strand.

The remaining four varieties are typically referred to as "wild silk" and are created from cocoons from which the pupa has emerged.

These silks are rougher and darker in color. They tend to be difficult to bleach and dye, but are prized for their naturally attractive appeal. Of these, muga or Assam silk, which is rich and golden in appearance, is arguable the most prized.

(Interestingly, India is the only place in the world where all five types of silk are produced.)

1) Mulberry Silkworm (Bombyx mori)

Although it is typically not necessary for the home sericulturist to draw the following distinctions, you should at least be aware of the fact that there are three groupings of "mulberry silkworms" separated by their breeding patterns.

- Univoltine silkworms are associated with European sericulture. The eggs of these worms are dormant during the winter and hatch in the spring.

- Bivoltine silkworms are found in China, Korea and Japan. They breed twice a year.

- Polyvoltine silkworms are indigenous to tropical climates, with eggs hatching in 9-12 days of being deposited. This allows for up to 8 lifecycles per year.

With the ability to purchase eggs from retailers, home sericulturists can raise silkworms year round and, if batches are staggered for hatching, on a continuous basis.

2) Tasar Silkworm (Antheraea mylitta)

Antheraea mylitta produces a coarse, copper-colored silk called Tasar or Tussah. The worms eat Asan and Arjun, plants indigenous to India, which is the principle area of production for this less lustrous variety of silk.

3) Oak Tasar Silkworm (Antheraea proyeli)

The *Antheraea proyeli* moth, a native of China, India, and Japan, feeds primarily on oak. The fiber it produces is also called tasar or tussah, but is of a finer quality.

4) Eri Silkworm (Philosamia ricini)

The caterpillars of *Philosamia ricini*, also present in India and throughout East Asia, eat castor leaves. The silk created from its cocoons is known as endi or errandi. These cocoons are open ended, making them unique in the world of sericulture.

The cocoons are not suitable for reeling, the standard method for harvesting silk from *Bombyx mori*. Instead, it is necessary for this fiber to be spun. The resulting thread is not glossy, but it is quite durable.

5) *Muga Silkworm (Antheraea assamensis)*

Antheraea assamensis is responsible for golden yellow muga silk made principally in the Indian state of Assam. The worms are also indigenous to China and Sri Lanka. They feed on ber, sal, som, oak, and fig plants.

Muga silk is used extensively in saris and other traditional Indian garments. The cocoons, which are almost as large as a hen's egg, are brown, and the fiber is glossy and fine.

The worms do not breed well in captivity, so the cocoons are harvested in the forest in their native environment, which is a major limitation on the spread of the muga silk industry.

B) The Unique Bombyx Mori

The "silkworm" is actually the larval stage of the silk moth's life cycle. Although these industrious caterpillars can eat the leaves of any mulberry tree, they prefer white mulberry leaves.

Bombyx mori can no longer be found in the wild and depends entirely on its relationship with humans for survival. Paradoxically, however, that existence is built on the worm's death.

Silkworms are carefully raised on a preferred diet of white mulberry leaves, and individually positioned to spin their silken cocoons with no overlap. However, before the pupa can emerge to become the silk moth, the cocoons are boiled to kill the creature inside.

Those precious cocoons are spun out of one, continuous, gossamer strand of silk. If the pupa were allowed to metamorphose into the moth, it would cut through the strand to escape, and the silk would be ruined, according to the traditional school of silk manufacture.

It should be noted, however, that there are viable methods of extracting silk fiber from broken cocoons. The resulting fabric has not usually been considered high quality. Today, as more environmentalists are calling for the humane production of silk, this view is changing.

Later in this book, I will discuss the production of "ahimsa" silk, which is made from cocoons from which the moth has been allowed to emerge.

Since this is a necessary part of sericulture (you do need adult moths to perpetuate your population), it may not be necessary to allow any cocoons to go to waste.

In the traditional view, however, *Bombyx mori* exists to give its life to the practice of sericulture, the breeding of silk worms for the express purpose of producing raw silk.

The worms don't have much to say about the whole process, which has been going on uninterrupted for at least five millennia.

C) The History of Sericulture

The Chinese discovered silk production around 2,700 BC. Over the centuries, the practice spread throughout China, but was unknown to the rest of the world until 139 BC when silken wares travelled from the Orient to Europe along the Silk Road.

1) A Modern Aside

Before we continue this brief history, I have to comment on a modern aside. If you use the Internet to further research sericulture and its associated tools and markets, you may type the phrase "silk road" into your favorite search engine at some point.

You will quickly be directed to information regarding an illegal drug site that was launched in 2011 and shut down by the Federal Bureau of Investigation in October 2013.

Reports indicate that this "Amazon" marketplace of the drug culture was re-launched in a "2.0" version shortly thereafter.

Additionally, there are online gaming communities that trade silk as a commodity or refer to "magic" silk or "glowing" silk. I found myself halfway through an article before I realized it was talking about gaming, not textile production!

I mention these issues so you don't waste your time looking at material that will be of no use to you, but also to help you avoid sites that could be unsafe to browse.

Be specific when searching for phrases. "Silk road trade route," for instance, will give you a wealth of information on the historic "highway" that linked the Eastern and Western worlds and brought silk to the royal houses of Europe.

2) The Ancient Silk Road

The historic Silk Road trade route, established during the Han Dynasty (206 BC to 220 CE) was the world's longest "highway" at the time, stretching from Eastern China all the way to the Mediterranean.

It covered more than 4,000 miles (6,437 kilometers) and served as a conduit not just for exotic goods, but for new ideas. Merchants and soldiers travelled its length, as did pilgrims and monks.

Although many kinds of goods made their way along the route, the Chinese were especially happy to sell their silk to the western world, where the fabric became a status symbol among royalty and wealthy nobles.

The Chinese were not, however, willing to give up the secret of how the gleaming fabric was produced. That riddle, they guarded with jealous secrecy.

The Romans, for instance, luxuriated in the silken fabrics, and entertained themselves by developing ludicrous theories about how the material was created. Some even went so far as to suggest that silk came from hairs combed from leaves.

In the third century, the Chinese finally lost their cherished silk monopoly when sericulture spread to Korea and then on to Japan.

Finally, in 522 AD, the Emperor Justinian discovered the truth -- silk was, as some waggish enthusiasts call it today -- "worm spit!"

The major European contributions to the silk industry were largely mechanical in nature, for instance improved weaving with power looms and the technology of roller printing. In 1801, a French inventor, Joseph Jacquard, developed a machine to perform figured silk weaving.

3) Pasteur and Pebrine

The real hero of European silk making, however, was none other than Louis Pasteur, the French chemist and microbiologist.

Pasteur developed the life-saving technique of vaccination that revolutionized the practice of medicine, but he also intervened in an epidemic that was killing silkworms in the south of France in 1865.

Pasteur unraveled the mystery of the transmission of Pebrine disease, which infects silkworm larvae, covering them in brown lesions and rendering them incapable of spinning their cocoons. The agent behind the infection is a microsporidian parasite, principally *Nosema bombycis*.

This deadly infection will kill 100% of the silkworms to hatch from an infected batch of eggs. The parasite lives on the leaves the silkworms eat, so it's contracted in the larval stage, passed to the adult moth, and then back to the next generation of eggs.

By instituting an inspection process to identify the disease in the moths after they laid their eggs, Pasteur created criteria for culling and destroying infected generations.

These inspections, performed under a microscope, are still used today to ensure that pebrine isn't passed down from the female moth to her offspring.

Although innovations and discoveries of this type led to a more mechanized and scientific approach to the making of silk, the industry has not thrived in every venue where it has been attempted, including America.

It is fair to say that sericulture has always followed the availability of mulberry leaves. (In the next chapter, I will discuss mulberry trees and shrubs at some length.)

Before the age of mass transit and the ability to purchase and ship mulberry leaves, silk making as an industry always failed to flourish in areas where a food source for the worms could not be stabilized.

4) Sericulture in the United States

As early as 1632, King James I of England tried to force the settlers of the Virginia Colony to plant mulberry trees in the New World and to cultivate silk worms as a cash industry.

The industrious colonists were enjoying considerable profits from the cultivation of tobacco, and resisted silk as too much hard work. Similar attempts failed in the southern colonies where another fiber industry, cotton, quickly gained ascendancy.

In 1826, Gideon B. Smith planted newly introduced Chinese mulberry trees in Ohio. Initially, the trees grew rapidly, and would-be silk manufacturers thrived there as well as in Connecticut, New Jersey, and Pennsylvania.

By 1840, however, this brief boom began to crash when it became apparent that the mulberry tree was simply not hardy enough to withstand American winters. A fatal blight struck the trees in 1844.

In *The Story of Silk and Cheney Silk*, by H.H. Manchester (1916), the author wrote:

"The fundamental reason [silk culture in America was abandoned] is not that mulberry trees and silkworms cannot with difficulty be raised in this country, but that the production of raw silk (cocoons) is essentially a household and hand process, still requiring, as in the days of ancient China, infinite patience and an disproportionate amount of human labor."

"Even in Italy, during the silkworm season, the whole house including the bedrooms and beds, is given over to the worms, upon which the women lavish every attention from daylight until late at night -- and for all this trouble and work, they ne   t only six or seven cents a day. In Japan and China, such household labor may bring as low as two or three cents a day."

The rapidly industrializing and profit conscious Americans were not attracted to an industry that thrived on the back of what Manchester described as "meagerly rewarded Oriental drudgery."

D) The Modern Silk Industry

Manchester's turn-of-the-century conclusion would seem to bear up 107 years later when you considered the major silk producing nations of the world. Essentially, the center of the silk industry remains firmly in place where it has always been – China, with India a close second.
For finished silk, the leaders are:

- China
- India
- Uzbekistan
- Brazil

- Japan
- Korea
- Thailand
- Vietnam
- Iran

For cocoons and raw silk:

- Kenya
- Botswana
- Nigeria
- Zambia
- Zimbabwe
- Bangladesh
- Colombia
- Egypt
- Japan
- Nepal
- Bulgaria
- Turkey
- Uganda
- Malaysia
- Romania
- Bolivia

The major silk consumers, however, are the United States, Italy, Japan, France, China, the United Kingdom, Switzerland, Germany, and the United Arab Emirates.

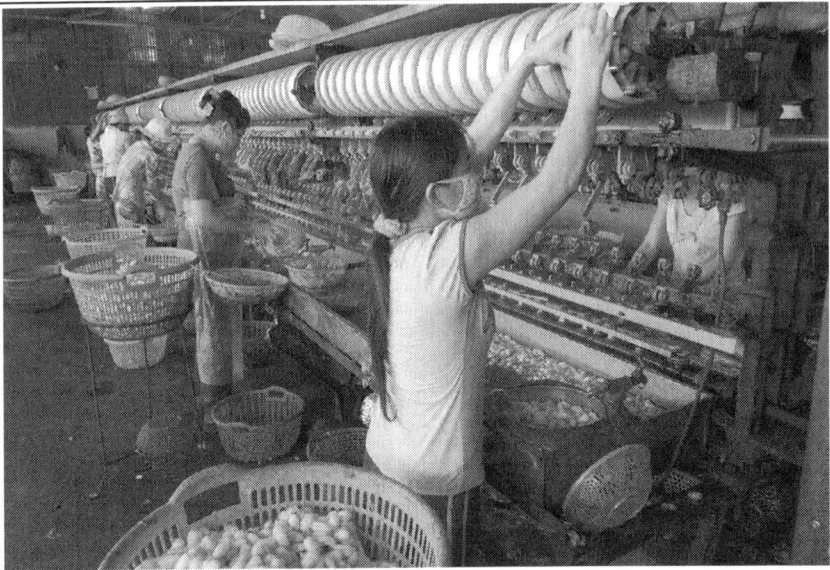

Today, more than 1 million Chinese workers are employed in the manufacture of silk, while 7.6 million labor lovingly over the worms and cocoons in India.

Some 20,000 families in Thailand weave silk, with sericulture considered a major mainstay of rural populations throughout Asia.

The work, although labor intensive, requires a minimal financial investment, while providing a raw textile that remains "evergreen" in terms of demand.

1) Silk for a New Age

As silk is a completely natural fiber, it is extremely environmentally friendly, but many critics, including the venerable Mahatma Ghandi, have long decried the fact that the silkworm must die for us to enjoy the gleaming material he produces.

Approximately 50,000 silkworms are killed to produce sufficient thread to weave a single silk sari! In an effort to counter this practice, seen as cruelty by many, "ahimsa" silk was developed.

Named for a religious principle advocating non-violence and a reverence for all life, moths used in the ahimsa process are allowed to escape the cocoon. The shell is then used to manufacture yarn.

This practice has spread among small manufacturers like Aurora Silk of Portland, Oregon (www.aurorasilk.com) that produces "peace" silk "from cocoons from which the moth has freely emerged to mate, lay eggs, and die happy. The eggs produced are then used in future generations of silk."

E) Raising Silkworms at Home

Individuals interested in raising silkworms at home do so for a variety of reasons.

1) Textile Production

Many are textile artisans who want to produce the fiber for use in their own creations.

There is certainly something unique in offering a product you have shepherded into existence through every step of the process.

These sericulturists lovingly raise the silkworms, harvest the cocoons, spin and dye the thread, and incorporate the fiber into projects involving everything from weaving to intricate embroidery.

In the sense that these works of art may then command good prices, it can be argued that these people are raising silkworms for profit, but obviously the chain of production is long and involved.

The time for the finished product to be offered for sale is considerable, and actually recouping your expenses is a tricky proposition at best.

2) Feeder Insects

People more directly interested in making money-raising silkworms, cultivate the creatures as pet food. Silkworms are highly nutritious feeder insects for reptiles, and once you have a pool of buyers, your demand should stay reasonably steady.

One woman who raises the worms for this purpose described her profit level as "grocery money." The trick is to maintain sufficient breeding stock in all stages of development to be able to meet your customer's needs.

Since silkworms go through four successive molts, they can be offered in sizes appropriate for the dietary needs of a wide variety of reptiles. This makes them highly versatile. Your major concerns will be volume and clientele.

3) Soap Making

An additional use or potential market for your raw silk is the production of homemade and boutique soaps. When dissolved in lye water, the protein present in the silk will give finished soaps a more lustrous sheen as well as enhanced lather.

Silk also lends a softer texture to soap, and the addition of the material is especially good for the "label" appeal of soap products destined for sale.

Silk's long-standing association with the concept of luxury is "transferrable" in the mind of consumers, but in this case, there is a definite change in the quality of the soap when the silk is added.

The soap making process requires very little silk fiber. For a 5 pound / 2.27 kg batch of soap, only an amount of silk equal to the size of a cotton ball is needed.

While this might not be a primary market for your home-based sericulture, sales to soap makers could be a good venue to dispose of the damaged cocoons created by the emergence of your breeding stock.

4) Pets and Projects

Finally, some people do choose to keep silkworms as pets, for the fascination of observing their lifecycle, and for their minimal space requirements. Insects or "mini beasts" of many types have become popular in recent years as pets.

Certainly you cannot interact with insects the same way you would with a dog or a cat, but you still have a living creature under your care, and one that can be more flexible in terms of its housing and care needs.

(If silk worms are not being raised for the production of silk, they can go as long as a week without food if they are well hydrated).

Husbanding silkworms is also an excellent project for children at home or as a class, so small scale sericulture "experiments" are popular in elementary school science classes and for home schooled children.

Any of these approaches to keeping silkworms at home can be taken on singly or in combination. *Bombyx mori* has lived with and been in service to man for thousands of years, and methods for its cultivation and care are well established and easily learned.

In the following chapters, we will look first at the basics of sericulture with the assumption that the worms are being kept to produce silk fiber, and then we will turn our attention to their needs when they are raised to be feeder insects.

F) Sericulture in Perspective

No discussion of sericulture would be complete without some consideration of the potential silkworm rearing offers impoverished populations around the world.

In less developed nations, or in backwaters of developed nations, sericulture is a low-cost option for a home-based industry with a conduit to a ready market.

In some cases, the profitability of sericulture depends on location and individual circumstances. What might not be success for some can be life changing for others. Consider the story of one woman in China who used sericulture to completely change not only her own destiny, but that of her village.

In the Chongqing Municipality of southwest China, a woman named Li Yifang from the village of Damiao Town was named one of Chongqing's "Ten Outstanding Women" in March 2013. She literally pulled herself out of poverty through sericulture.

Some thirty years ago, Li's family owned less than an acre of land. Li borrowed money to start raising silkworms. In

1992, her business was doing well enough that she borrowed $1,609 / £978 from the bank and another $1,287 / £782 from friends and family to plant mulberry trees to expand her operations.

For the next year, Li worked tirelessly from dawn to dusk raising the leaves her worms consumed. Even though she was still in debt, she hired fellow villagers to assist her with her operations.

She faced many hardships, including the loss of many of her worms and much of her capital to an improper use of fertilizer. Her husband, frustrated and angry over the setbacks, left to find work elsewhere. Li persevered and increased her working knowledge of sericulture, taking a government sponsored course.

The decision to stick with sericulture proved a good one. Li began to make money, which she reinvested. In 2000, she was able to move her family into a new home where she now teaches other villagers how to raise silkworms and claw their way out of poverty aided by the same industrious worms that changed her life.

This is but one story among many that illustrate the power of the silkworm to partner with its human keepers in a profitable endeavor. In the developed world, sericulture's impact tends to be less dramatic, but regardless, the relationship the silkworm enjoys with humans is unique and fascinating.

Chapter 2) - Silk as a Fiber

It is a misconception to regard silk as a "delicate" fiber, a stereotype that developed from the material's association with luxury and fine items.

One of the reasons silk is popular as a material for men's neckties, for instance, is its ability to withstand the friction and pressure of being repeatedly knotted and unknotted.

Silk is smooth and soft with a natural sheen. It is not, however, "slippery" like satin, which is a high gloss weave often confused with silk. Although silk can be used to produce a soft, high luster satin, the latter is not a distinct fabric in and of itself.

Silk can withstand up to 177 pounds / 80.3 kg of force before breaking. By comparison, wool, another natural fiber, will tear at just 20 pounds / 9 kg of force. Silk is actually stronger than one of the most popular synthetic fabrics, denim, which will tear with 164 pounds / 74 kg of force. (Silk is more prone to break when wet).

In terms of elasticity, silk can be stretched 1/5th /5.08 mil to 1/7th / 3.55 mil of an inch before breaking. Over time, the material loses its elasticity if subject to continuous pulling, however, and becomes misshapen.

Silk also resists heat well, remaining largely unaffected at temperatures up to 284 F / 140 C. It will, however, begin to

decompose at 347 F / 175 C and degrades when left exposed
to sunlight for long periods of time.

Garments made of silk are generally "dry clean only" or
should be hand washed. Chlorine bleach should never be
used with silk, and women should allow their hairspray
and perfume to dry before they put on silk clothing.
One should hand wash silk in lukewarm water with a mild
soap that does not contain alkaline. A small amount of
distilled white vinegar in the rinse water will dissolve any
soap residue left in the fabric.

Never "wring out" silk or twist the fabric. Instead, roll the
material inside an absorbent towel to remove excess water
after washing.

Putting silk items of any kind in a washing machine is strongly discouraged, even on the delicate cycle and with the use of a mesh bag for protection.

Silk garments can be hung up to dry. The material won't stretch. Do not, however, allow silk to dry in direct sunlight.

Minor wrinkles in silk will disappear if the material is hung overnight. To remove stubborn wrinkles, use an iron with a "silk" setting or hang the silk garment in the bathroom while you shower. The humidity will remove the wrinkles without damaging the fabric.

A) Understanding Grades of Silk

The quality of many fabrics is described by a system of "thread count." This grading scheme is not used with silks, which are rated in part by their weight. The figure or "momme" (pronounced "mummy") is a numerical value followed by the abbreviation "mm."

Momme is a description in pounds of the weight of a 100-yard length of silk that is 45 inches wide. Therefore, 100 yards of an 8mm silk will weighs 8 pounds. (This is a very common silk fabric weight for dresses and clothing).

Higher quality silks will fall in a momme range of 14-16mm+, while silks used in bedding and upholstery may be 19mm or more.

The greater the momme weight assigned to a silk fabric, the heavier and more opaque it will be, while a lower momme weight may be so sheer as to be "see through." Some typical momme values are:

- charmeuse 12-22mm
- chiffon 6-8mm
- crepe de chine 3-5mm
- gauze 8-12mm
- georgette 5-16mm
- habutai 4-6mm
- organza 35-40mm

B) Types of Silk Fabrics

There are many types of silk fabric commonly used for clothing, upholstery, household items like bedding, and a wide range of other applications. The following are some of the most popular.

1) Chiffon

Chiffon is a lightweight silk that is often described as "diaphanous." The material is translucent and tends to billow when used in a garment. Generally, chiffon requires a lining when used for clothing and is a popular choice for scarves.

2) China Silk

China silk is also a sheer, lightweight fabric. You may also see it referred to as pongee, habotai, or habutai. China silk is both common and inexpensive. It is too light to use in fitted garments and is often used to make scarves.

3) Crepe de Chine

Crepe de Chine is a lightweight silk variety in which some of the fibers are twisted clockwise while others are turned counter- clockwise.

The weaving style is plain, but the twist of the fiber gives the finished product a pebbled surface. Crepe de Chine is very soft and will tear if handled roughly, therefore it is not used in clothing designs that are highly structured.

4) Charmeuse

Charmeuse is the ubiquitous fabric that most people envision when they hear the word "silk." The anterior side of the material is flat in appearance, while the front shimmers with a satin-like weave.

Charmeuse drapes beautifully and is used in a wide range of clothing styles from lingerie to blouses and evening clothes. It is regarded as one of the most beautiful of all fabrics and is synonymous with an image of luxury.

5) Douppioni

Plain woven douppioni has a tafetta-like stiffness and is typically dyed in bright hues. This type of silk is often used in semi-fitted gentleman's vests as well as in evening gowns for ladies.

Douppioni does not stand up well to stress and must be dry cleaned to avoid damaging abrasions to the weave.

6) Gauze

Gauze is an extremely sheer form of silk made of fine, but very strong, threads. The material's stability is strengthened by the weave, which interlocks and is often referred to as a "leno structure." This prevents the shifting of the threads, thus reducing the tendency to tear, pull, or fray.

Silk gauze is most often used as a lining or facing and is popular as a very fine needlepoint canvas. When used as a needlepoint canvas, the gauze may also carry an HPI (hole per inch) rating.

7) Georgette

Georgette, named for the French dressmaker and designer Georgette de la Plante, is a lightweight silk with a dull finish, much like crepe. It is created with yarns that have been twisted to create a crinkled surface in "S" and "Z" patterns.

Available in both solids and prints, silk Georgette is used in dresses, evening gowns, blouses, and as a trimming. It has a "springier" texture than chiffon, to which it is closely related, and so lends a completely different look when incorporated in fashion designs.

8) Jacquard

Jacquard is a woven silk fabric with a contrasting weave of matte and highly reflective threads that create light and dark counter effects.

The material closely resembles brocade, but only a single color is used in Jacquard patterns. The material is heavier than most silks and is densely woven in floral and paisley patterns.

9) Noil

Short fibers left after silk has been combed and carded are gathered up to create noil, which lacks the traditional shine associated with most silks.

Noil more closely resembles cotton, but has a very soft feel and drapes well without wrinkling, making it a popular choice for travel garments.

10) Raw Silk

Any silk yarn or fabric that has not been "de-gummed" to remove the natural binding sericin is described as "raw." Fabric produced from these fibers will be both stiff and dull, with a tendency to hold odors and attract dirt.

11) *Shantung*

Modern shantung is typically made from silk worm yarns and heavy douppioni filling yarns. The fabric tends to be firm and crisp, but it unravels easily and does not work well in close-fitting styles. The sheen may be either dull or lustrous.

12) *Tussah*

Also called shantung, tussah silk is produced from wild silk worms. It is much more coarse than more refined silks and resists dying. Tussah's natural color, however, is a pleasing creamy tan, which accounts for its popularity.

Because of tussah's tendency to ravel, the fabric should be dry cleaned only, but is an excellent material for travel garments because it does not wrinkle easily.

13) *Organza*

Organza is a plain, sheer fabric traditionally made from silk, although some modern variants may include synthetic fibers like nylon or polyester.

Organza is often used in wedding gowns and evening wear, and is also a popular fabric for interior decorating treatments like heavy draperies.

Chapter 3) – Basics of Sericulture

At least in terms of spinning the raw silk, your silk worms will, if fed and housed properly, do all the work for you. It is at the point that you harvest the cocoons that you will actually begin working with the silk. This may mean:

- Selling the intact cocoons to someone else to be unraveled and spun into thread.
- Harvesting the fiber yourself and selling it.
- Harvesting and spinning the fiber into thread.
- Harvesting, spinning, and dying the thread.

Perhaps you will sell the dyed thread or use if for weaving and embroidery. The options from an artistic standpoint are limited only by your imagination and talent.

Before you can make any of those decisions, however, you must understand the basics of silkworm husbandry as they apply to actually making silk.

A) The Silkworm Lifecycle

Depending on the intended purpose or your sericulture project, you will interrupt the lifecycle of some of your silkworms either by killing the pupa in the cocoon or by using the caterpillars as reptile feed before a cocoon is spun.

(The worms, which can grow to 3 inches / 7.62 cm in length are ideal feeder insects. Silkworms move slowly, they go through four distinct molts and are thus useful in a variety of sizes, and they do not bite).

In order to maintain your "livestock," however, regardless of why the worms are being raised, you will always allow some individuals to mature, mate, and produce the next generation.

The broad phases of the lifecycle are as follows:

- A female *Bombyx mori* moth lays masses of tiny eggs.
- The eggs hatch, and tiny black caterpillars emerge.
- The caterpillars feed on mulberry leaves and grow.
- Through four successive moltings they reach maturity.

This stage of the silkworm's development lasts between 4 and 6 weeks. At the end of the larval stage, each worm begins to spin its silk cocoons so it will have a safe space to pupate. This process requires about 3 days.

At this point, one of two things will happen. Either the cocoon will be immersed in hot water to kill the pupa and enable the undamaged thread to be unwound, or the pupa will be allowed to emerge after three weeks.

If the pupa is allowed to emerge as a new moth, those adults form the foundation of your breeding stock, but they will be with you only a few days.

Adult silk moths do not have functional mouths. They exist only to mate. The males die first, and then the females die after having deposited their eggs. The moths also lack the ability to fly, so they are easily managed. Each female deposits 200-500 lemon yellow eggs that then turn black.

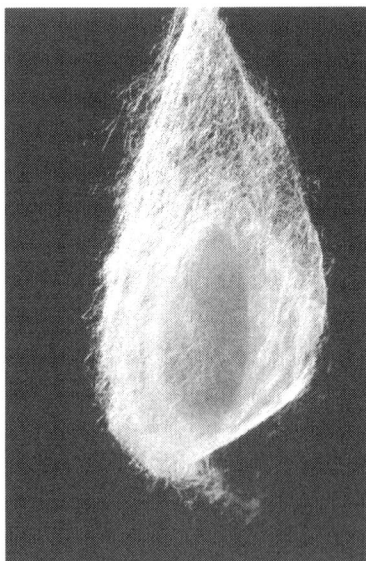

Time estimates for the total lifecycle are:

- 31 days in the larval stage
- 10 days in the pupa stage
- 5 days in the adult stage

This means that you should be able to harvest one "crop" of silk per batch of eggs approximately once a month. (It is highly recommended that you keep a detailed journal of your first few batches. Silkworms are highly responsive to their environment. You should be able to work out fairly exact time tables unique to your individual set up and environment).

You can, of course, increase your production by staggering the lifecycle and constantly keeping your silkworms in varying stages of development.

Your production will be limited primarily by space considerations, and your ability to locate food for your silkworms.

Many beginning sericulturists describe their considerable shock at just how much silkworms eat, and how vigorously. If you have enough worms, the noise from their chewing sounds very like a rain shower!

B) What Is Silk?

One of the most remarkable things about a silkworm's cocoon is that it is comprised of a single continuous thread that reaching lengths of 984-2953 feet / 300-900 meters.

Each worm has two salivary glands located on either side of its head. These glands secrete the liquid protein from which the silk is made.

When a cocoon is harvested, gaining access to the silk fiber is as simple as using proven techniques to unwind the thread, which is completely natural.

C) Buying Silkworm Eggs

Obviously your first step in beginning silk production at home is to acquire *Bombyx mori* eggs. They are generally available from suppliers from late spring into the fall, which corresponds with the time the mulberry trees have their leaves.

Some suppliers use artificial foods, however, and so are able to sell eggs year round. If you request that eggs be shipped with an ice pack via overnight delivery, you can refrigerate the eggs for up to a month to keep them in a dormant state until all your equipment is in place.

The recommended temperature for refrigeration is 35-37 F / 1.6-2.7 C at 70-80% humidity.

When you allow the eggs to come up to room temperature, they will hatch within 8-10 days. Healthy silkworm eggs are roughly the size of a poppy seed. They are blue-gray to black and have a tiny dimple in the middle

Obviously you do not want to allow the eggs to hatch until you are certain you have a food source for the caterpillars.

D) Estimated Cost of Silkworm Eggs

Estimated Costs:

Glued down in a petri dish
200     $9.49
1000 $20.99

Loose in bulk
2000 $20.00

E) Feeding Your Silkworms

The food you choose for your silkworms will affect the quality of the silk they produce. In this chapter, I'm assuming you will be cultivating the insects for their fiber, so there's really only one food source you need to locate — the leaves of mulberry trees or bushes.

If you want silk thread that is snowy white, extremely strong, and with a beautiful sheen, feed your silkworms only white mulberry leaves.

This species, *Morus alba,* is the principle food that has been used in Chinese sericulture for thousands of years.

1) Locating Mulberry Trees

Mulberry trees and bushes do best in a temperate climate. Both plants are, however, cultivated throughout a fairly large geographic region extending from the tropical zone

45

into much cooler climates.

The plants, not surprisingly, enjoy the widest distribution in the Far East, the birthplace of sericulture. Mulberries are plentiful in China, Japan, and Korea as well as in South East Asia.

It is possible, however, to find mulberries in Brazil, as well as in Italy, Spain, Greece, and even the south of France. In the United States, mulberries can be found from New England to the Midwest and down to the Gulf Coast.

Some varieties thrive in the hotter, more arid climate of the American Southwest, while others prefer the humid Hawaiian Islands.

The best soil for mulberries, regardless of geographic region, is deep and light with a rich or sandy texture and excellent natural drainage. Mulberries will not grow in wet or damp soil.

2) *Varieties of Mulberry*

Understand, however, that just because mulberry trees will grow in a region, there's no guarantee the silkworms will be content to dine on the local fare. The worms can be quite particular about what they eat.

- As a general rule, silkworms will not eat *Morus rubra*, the Red Mulberry, which is too acidic for their tastes.

- Silkworms will eat the leaves of *Morus nigra*, the black mulberry, but they do so with difficulty because the foliage is prickly.

- Philippine mulberry, *Morus multicaulis*, which is a shrub, is less nutritious than other varieties, but it can be cultivated easily, grows back rapidly, and the worms will eat it.

There are actually several varieties of the venerable white mulberry, the best known being *Morus Moretti* and *Morus alba rosea*.
Not only will a diet of white mulberry produce the finest silk, the trees often exceed 50 feet / 15.24 meters in height and are easily propagated from cuttings, layers, and seeds.

3) *Mulberry Leaves*

Mulberry trees or bushes are often found in city parks, cemeteries, churchyards, and private yards. It's to your advantage to learn to recognize the plants on sight and to identify what's available in your area before you begin to raise silkworms.

Other silkworm enthusiasts can help you to determine the dietary suitability of any mulberry source you locate. You may want to photograph both the living tree or shrub and a sample of the leaves to aid with identification.

You need to know if silkworms will eat the plants in question, what, if any, effect the diet will have on the quality of the silk, and if you can have access to the leaves as a food source.

Do all of this in advance of ordering silkworms or silkworm eggs. If you don't have a reliable food source for your purposes, there's no point in continuing!

When you do locate local mulberry trees or shrubs, always secure permission to gather the leaves from the owner of the property. At the same time, find out if the plant has been sprayed with insecticides or if any such treatment is planned in the future.

4) Picking Mulberry Leaves

Be forewarned that silkworms eat a lot. In order to get enough leaves to feed 25 caterpillars, you'll require access to the leaves from two medium-sized trees or two large bushes.

(Don't forget to multiply the available food supply versus projected number of worms any time you decide to expand your operation).

When you gather food for your silkworms, pick only the leaves, not the branches and don't strip a tree. Harvesting only the leaves will encourage new ones to take their place.

You can keep fresh leaves in the refrigerator in "zippered" plastic bags for approximately 5 days. Remember that while leaves may look fine to you after that length of time, the determining factor in their suitability for the worms is moisture.

Only fresh mulberry leaves have enough moisture to not only keep your silkworms fed, but also well hydrated.

If there is a mulberry tree in an area to which you don't have routine access, you may ask to take a small branch. Explain that you raise silkworms and often have trouble finding food for them.

Ask if there is a branch you may take that won't harm the appearance of the tree. If the owner agrees, you can keep a branch in water for up to a week.

Do not, however, put your caterpillars on a branch that is being kept alive in water. They'll fall off and drown!

5) Artificial Foods

It's also possible to order artificial food online, but these diets do not always allow the worms to produce good quality silk.

This is a matter of some debate among enthusiasts, with many saying there is no appreciable difference in the fiber. The judgment may, in the end, be a matter of personal taste and preference.
Again, this is a topic you will want to investigate by talking to other sericulturists who have had experience with the product in question.

(See the section at the back of the book on Relevant Websites for silkworm communities you may join).

Most artificial foods are made of powdered mulberry leaves and are mixed with water for use. Some suppliers also offer mulberry "chow," which is comprised of chopped or loose leaves. Keeping this type of product fresh can be difficult, however.

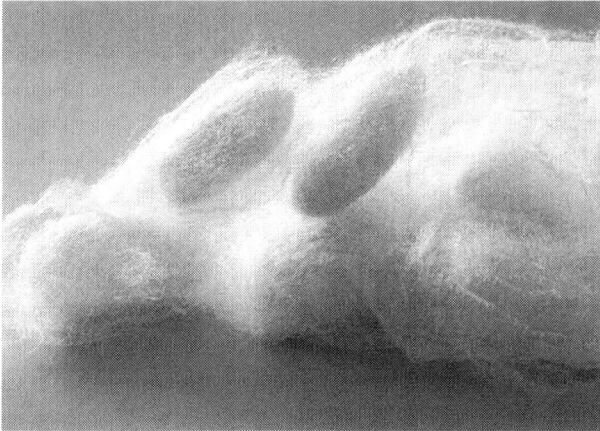

There are anecdotal reports that silkworms eating artificial powdered foods may not spin cocoons at all, while other sericulturists report that their livestock accepts the food with a normal appetite.

If you are producing worms to serve as feeder insects, you do not need to worry about the cocoons, but it is important to be aware of potential problems with artificial foods if you are attempting to harvest silk fiber.

Silkworms that have been receiving a diet of fresh mulberry leaves may reject powdered food when it is first offered to them. Placing the food on green lettuce leaves will help the worms to make the transition, and will keep the artificial food moist.

Artificial foods will keep for as much as a year in powdered form, and for two months when mixed with water and stored in the refrigerator.

Obviously such foods offer tremendous flexibility to the sericulturist, provided the preparations meet your goals for raising your worms in the first place.

Refer to Chapter 7 for the estimated costs associated with artificial foods.

6) Feeding Techniques for a New Age

For five millennia the standard in sericulture has been enticing worms to spin pristine white thread to be used in high end luxury fabrics. Silk of this caliber, from its earliest introduction, has been regarded as a status symbol. Traditionally, the pure white silk has been dyed across a wide range of brilliant hues, a process that now troubles environmentally-minded artisans. Particularly when produced in large scale, the dying process creates toxic wastewater.

In December 2013, a group of scientists published their findings in the journal *ACS Sustainable Chemistry & Engineering*. Their innovative contribution to the world of sericulture is the attempt to have silkworms produce "pre-dyed" silk by feeding them dyed mulberry leaves.

Currently, the technique has only been tried with a single color and is far too expensive to be implemented on a wide scale.

The experiment does show, however, that far from being a "dead" art form, sericulture continues to evolve and to be refined more than 5,000 years after its initial discovery.

If the feeding technique can be perfected and widely implemented, it would no doubt add another fascinating level of creativity to an already old and well-developed art form.

F) Housing and Rearing Silkworms

When you purchase silkworm eggs from a supplier, they typically arrive in either a petri dish or attached to a piece of paper.

At the stage of production where you are hatching eggs laid by your own moths, the eggs will be attached to the liner you've chosen for the egg-laying box. Many home sericulturists find that freezer paper works quite well for this purpose.

Keep your silkworms in a warm room where the temperature is between 78-88 F / 26-31 C to get the fastest growth rate.

1) Eggs in the Hatching Box

Silkworm eggs hatch within two weeks of the time they are removed from cold storage. Most commercial suppliers ship eggs mid-way through this period, so the tiny kegos ("hairy babies") should emerge about a week after you receive them.

At hatching, the worms will be the size of small brown ants. By some internal clock we don't understand, the eggs almost always hatch at dawn, and all on the same day.

Any small box that will contain the kegos is fine. Once they are supplied with mulberry leaves, they only let go of the current leaf to crawl on to another so it's quite easy to transfer the population to a larger enclosure as necessary.

You will be surprised that the worms eagerly anticipate their feedings, waving their heads around and reaching for the leaves they are given. Put the leaves directly on top of the worms. They won't go looking for them!

2) Begin with a Small Rearing Box

Once the eggs have hatched, the tiny caterpillars must eat within 4 hours. If they are not provided with mulberry leaves, they will die of dehydration. Bear in mind that silkworms grow at an incredible rate and they must have a constant supply of food.

Replace the leaves at least 3 times a day, so that the worms have a supply that is both fresh and moist. Silkworms don't drink water. All their moisture must come from fresh mulberry leaves. This is crucial to their survival.

Do not, however, give your worms leaves that are damp. If silkworms ingest mold from their food, they will die. Be very vigilant about watching their leaves for any sign of mold growth.

A small box lined with paper and outfitted with a screened or vented lid serves well as a rearing box. Try not to go smaller than 6" x 6" / 15.24 cm x 15.24 cm and make sure there is no way for the worms to fall out.

3) Progress to a Large Rearing Box

Silkworms grow rapidly during the one-month larval stage, increasing their body size approximately 10,000 times. The first molt typically occurs within 4 days of hatching.

You will know the worms are about to shed their skins because they will stop eating for several hours and sit perfectly still with their heads in an upright position. After the first molt, the worms will by gray and have very smooth skin.

With each molt, the worms' heads get larger, and their body color gets lighter and lighter until they are pure white. As they grow, they begin to eat continuously day and night. You must monitor their food supply constantly.

After the first molt, you'll want to move the worms into a larger rearing box that is at least 12" x 24" / 31 cm x 61 cm or larger depending on how many silkworms you are tending.

It's a good idea to select a loosely woven basket at this stage of the worms' growth. The slats will allow the excrement or "fass" to fall through. The openings should not be large enough for the worms themselves to get stuck or to escape. If you use a container with a solid bottom and paper lining, the fass must be cleaned out every day.

After the last molt, the worms begin to use their energy to build silk protein for spinning their cocoons rather than increasing their body mass.

The thorax or "chest" region starts to increase in size, and the worms begin to wave their heads around, signaling their instinctual desire to start their cocoons.

If you are not careful, the worms will try to crawl out of the rearing box to find a place to spin. Now is the time to move them into a spinning box, and to instigate a policy of segregation.

4) The Magic of the Spinning Box

Your spinning box should be at least as large as the rearing box, and you will definitely want a vented or screened lid.

Try to use clear plastic so you can watch the worms at work; it's a fascinating process!

The ventilation not only prevents potential escape, but it also makes sure there's good air flow around the cocoons. The worms must be segregated in their own little spaces within the box so they can create their cocoons in isolation of one another.

If the cocoons are allowed to touch, the fibers will become tangled, and it will be impossible to separate them. Use egg cartons in the bottom of the box, or cut the tubes from toilet tissue or paper towels into small round chambers, placing one worm in each segment.

Obviously if you are cultivating a large number of worms, you're going to need multiple spinning boxes. Don't scrimp on space in this stage of the process. It's imperative that the worms have enough room to spin their cocoons without touching one another.

The individual cocoons are long and oval with slight indentions in the center. They will range in color from snowy white to golden yellow.
The worms secrete two proteins during the spinning process: fibroin and sericin. The strand of silk is made of fibroin, while the sericin is the "gum" that holds the coiled strands together.

When the cocoons are "degummed" in a bath prior to being unraveled, the sericin is removed, freeing the long, continuous thread of fibroin. It is also possible, however, to process the silk with the sericin in place, removing it later before spinning or weaving.

5) Deciding How to Use the Cocoons

If you intend to harvest the cocoons for silk, the cocoons are "stifled" with heat or steam to kill the pupa. This allows the fiber to be reeled off, providing the finest silk.

If the pupa is allowed to emerge, the silk can still be spun, but it will not be of the same quality.

If cocoons are not stifled, within two weeks the moth inside will begin to secrete a brown liquid to soften the surface so it can push its way out to freedom.

When the adult or imago, emerges, it is covered in soft fuzz and does not have the ability to fly.

The males use special receptors on their antenna to detect females at a distance of several hundred feet. Within a few hours, mating occurs and the females lay their eggs.

The adults die soon thereafter since they have no working mouths and can't eat.

6) Transferring to the Breeding Box

If you allow adults to emerge from the cocoons, transfer them to a breeding box that is approximately 12" x 24" / 31 cm x 61 cm and outfitted with a vented lid.

For breeding purposes, select the largest and firmest cocoons. You should also allow any soiled cocoons to hatch, since the fiber is already ruined.

Line the bottom of the box with freezer paper so the female's eggs will adhere to the surface.

Once the eggs have been deposited, you are ready to begin the whole process again!

7) Successful Silkworm Cultivation Requires

If you are to be successful in cultivating silkworms, make sure that:

- **You keep the worms in clean conditions**. Silkworms are extremely susceptible to infection, and to fungal growth among other serious potential issues. The cleaner their living circumstances, the better.

- **The area around the worms is well ventilated, but with a uniform temperature.** Air flow is essential, but the ambient temperature needs to remain constant for the worms to thrive. Strive for 75-80 F / 24-27 C.

- **The worms are not to be kept in crowded conditions.** This is especially important when they begin to spin their cocoons. If the worms are too near one another, the cocoons will become intertwined and it will be impossible to separate out the silk.

- **The worms receive a constant food supply.** Silkworms should never go without a ready source of food except when they are molting. At those times, the choice to not eat is their own. Otherwise, they should have an uninterrupted food source.

- **Worms of the same age are housed together.** If you want to accurately supervise the silkworm's lifecycle to anticipate molting and the spinning of the cocoons, it's essential that hatches of eggs not be intermingled. Silkworms of an equal age will mature at an equal rate.

In the beginning, work with a modest number of eggs and take copious notes. Don't undertake a large batch of silkworms until you've raised a small group through the entire lifecycle successfully and harvested your first silk.

Most beginning sericulturists need about a year of experience to learn, mainly through trial and error, what does and does not work in their unique set up. Only when you are able to consistently raise silkworms and harvest the cocoons should you consider expanding your operation. Set realistic goals for yourself in terms of production. If you have, for instance, 3.5-4 lbs. / 1.58-1.81 kg of dry cocoons, they will yield approximately 1 lb. / 0.45 kg of raw silk.

A single cocoon will yield as much as 800-1500 yards / 731.5-1371.6 meters of thread!

Chapter 4) – Working with Silk Fiber

There are actually many ways to work with raw silk. For the purposes of an introduction to basic sericulture, this chapter will primarily explore "reeling," which is the process of taking a silkworm cocoon from its natural state as a tight little oval bundle to a length of shining silk fiber.

At the end of the chapter, however, I will discuss attenuating or spreading out cocoons. Understand that when you take up sericulture, the fundamental steps only open the door to what may well be years of perfecting your craft.

For many people, this is the great pleasure of working with silkworms. The little worms will continue to teach you new lessons for as long as they are a part of your life.

For the process of unreeling, you will want to work on a well-protected surface since the cocoons drip, and wet fragments of silk will tend to coat everything you're using. Be sure to have plenty of towels on hand, as well as large slotted spoons and forks.

A) Preparing the Cocoons

The cocoons are placed in hot water to kill the pupa inside. The water should be simmering, not boiling. Use the slotted spoon to hold the cocoons underwater. They will "fizz" for a brief period of time as the inside air is expelled and the material is beginning to soften.

Some sericulturists begin by soaking the cocoons in hot tap water, then transferring them to cold water, then back to a pan of water brought to a boil and removed from the stove.

With each cocoon, you must find the start of the thread. With the cocoons floating in the water, stir the surface with a small dish brush to begin to pick up loosened strands of silk.

Some cocoons will simply drop away, but when you have collected several and have their true ends, transfer them to a separate bowl with the ends of the filaments draped over the edge. It's useful to place a damp paper towel over the edge of the bowl so the silk fibers will stick to it.

You will want batches of approximately 12-15 cocoons to begin reeling. Capture the filament from each cocoon and cast it on to the reeler. The cocoons should sit in a bowl of water during this process.

B) Reeling the Silk

For the home sericulturist, the most challenging piece of equipment to acquire is a silk reeler. There are many styles of reelers. In large silk factories, powered reelers are outfitted with multiple frames to increase production volume.

For home use, you are looking for a device that will allow you to unreel the strands of silk as well as to separate and hold them for drying. One of the most efficient devices for this purpose is also the most difficult to find, a Japanese zakuri.

A zakuri is a hand-cranked device that draws the thread onto a large bobbin. The complete measurements for a zakuri are available at www.wormspit.com/zakuri. This authoritative site has a wealth of information for home sericulturists.

The site's owner suggests that a wood worker could take the provided dimensions and reproduce the design of the zakuri, which was mass produced in large quantities in Japan in the 19th century. Although an ideal solution, zakuris are almost impossible to find.

Another option is a tavalette or croissure, a device used widely by sericulturists in Laos. Unfortunately, they are just as difficult to find and are often custom-made for the textile artisans who use them.

(To see a tavalette or croissure used in the process of silk reeling, please visit www.blue-room.com/onetruth/archive/2010/05/silk-reeling.html.)

An easier and more readily available solution is a clock reel yarn winder like the one pictured here. These simple units are hand cranked and do a good job of keeping the raw silk fiber securely in place and untangled before spinning.

Wooden clock reelers often show up on eBay for around $250 / £153. They can also be ordered from craftsmen who manufacture spinning wheels. Prices will vary widely by source.

Regardless of its form, the reel serves as a frame to separate the strands. As you turn the crank, you can watch the cocoons spin in the bowl as the fibers come off.

When the pupa becomes visible inside each cocoon, you have reached the end of that length of fiber. It may take as much as 45 minutes of reeling to completely remove all the silk from your cocoons.

To spin the unreeled strand into thread, cut the fiber into five-inch / 12.7 cm lengths. They will be stiff because via this method, the sericin is still coating the silk. The fibers need to be degummed.

C) Degumming Silk

Place the lengths of silk in a hot bath of equal parts soap and washing soda. Turn the heat down to simmer and leave the fiber in the bath for 30 minutes. Do not prod or stir the silk as this will cause it to tangle.

After 30 minutes, pour the fiber and water into a colander and rinse the silk under running water. Clean the pot and fill it with one gallon / 3.8 liters of water to which a teaspoon / 5 grams of vinegar has been added.

Let the silk to sit in the vinegar for a few minutes before again pouring the fiber into the colander and rinsing. Allow the silk to dry on dish towels.

The next logical step at this point of the production is to use one of several spinning methods to create silk thread from the lengths of dried silk.

D) Spinning / Weaving Silk

Spinning is itself an art form and one in which you will require hands on training. There are several methods, including the use of a spindle, a treadle, or a spinning wheel, among others.

Most artisans who are sufficiently dedicated to their craft to go to the trouble of raising their own silkworms will know how to spin, dye, and weave well in advance of beginning sericulture.

If, however, you are starting completely from scratch, the following books will help you to learn these ancillary crafts to the art of silk making. I also highly recommend that you take classes or attend workshops to acquire these skills.

Spinning

- Carol Kross, *The Whole Craft of Spinning from Raw Material to Finished Yarn*

- Abby Franquemont, *Respect the Spindle: Spin Infinite Yarns with One Amazing Tool*

- Maggie Casey, *Start Spinning*

- Jacey Boggs, *Spin Art: Mastering the Craft of Spinning*

Weaving

- Deborah Chandler, *Learning to Weave*

- Madelyn van der Hoogt, *The Weaver's Companion*

- Peggy Osterkamp, *Weaving for Beginners*
- Candace Crockett, *Card Weaving*

Dyeing

- Rita Buchanan, *A Dyer's Garden*

- Kate Broughton, *Textile Dyeing: The Step-by-Step Guide*
- Ashley Martineau, *Spinning and Dyeing Yarn*

- Gene Shepherd, *Prepared to Dye: Dying Techniques for Fiber Artists*

E) Marketing Raw Silk

It is not out of the question to market the product of your sericulture at any stage of the process. The trick is to find a local market to which you can cater. You might:

- Raise your silkworms and allow them to spin their cocoons, which you will then sell after having killed the pupa. Your customers would then harvest the silk for their own purposes.

- Follow the process to the point of reeling the raw silk, which you would then sell to a craftsman for spinning into thread or yarn.

- Spin and dye the thread yourself, offering it for sale to weavers and other textile artisans.

It is extremely difficult to be able to achieve a high production volume when making silk at home. However, if you generate extremely high quality silk fiber or silk thread, you may develop a cottage industry supported by other local crafters.

For instance, you might find that you could sell your raw silk or silk threads at renaissance fairs, which are role-playing venues that are also dedicated to preserving many ancient arts from calligraphy and paper making to weaving and tapestry production.

It's impossible to guess what you might be able to earn, since local circumstances will vary widely. Before you undertake such a venture, contact local craft groups to explore your potential market.

F) Mawatas, an Alternate Method

Working with silk in this way, each cocoon is made into a single silk square or mawata. The word translates from Japanese to English as "to spread around." You will also see these referred to as "hankies" Follow these steps:

- Place your cocoons in a slow cooker for 30-45 minutes in a mixture of 1 gallon / 2.8 liters of water, 1/4 cup of paste soap, and 1/4 cup of washing soap.

- Hold the cocoons down in the mixture to prevent floating.

The purpose of the bath is to dissolve the sericin holding the fibers together.

- When the cocoons are pliable enough to easily lose their shape, but still maintain their physical integrity (rather than turning to mush) they're ready to go.

- Gently nudge an opening in the end of the wet cocoon with your fingers. Don't break the fibers! Be careful. The cocoon will be hot and may contain hot liquid. Your goal is to remove the pupa.

- Slowly begin to work the cocoon with your fingers, stretching out the fibers until you are able to hook one end over an 8" x 8" / 20.3 cm x 20.3 cm frame with posts in the corners to hold the material secure. (This is the type of "stretcher" frame typically used in needlepoint and cross-stitch projects.)

- Continue working with the cocoon until all four corners are secure. Repeat the process with 9 more cocoons so you have a total of 10 layers on the frame.

- Hold the frame under a stream of water in the sink and rinse the stretched material thoroughly. Do not rub the stack, or the fibers will become tangled.

- Rinse again with a mild citric acid solution to remove any washing soda residue, and then rinse with a fabric softener formulated for silk.

- Gently remove the stack from the frame. Place it between two layers of paper towels. Roll the towels and squeeze the material dry.

- Hang the stack up to allow for thorough drying.

Mawatas are suitable for spinning on a drop spindle, a very old and simple method for creating yarn.

Chapter 5) – Silkworms as Feeder Insects

Silkworms make an ideal feeder insect for reptiles and amphibians for a number of reasons. Silkworms:

- have high nutritional value
- don't bite
- are soft-bodied and slow moving
- can be fed to achieve a desired size

Additionally, silkworms grow quickly, reaching their maximum length of 3 inches / 7.62 cm in 25-28 days.

A) Housing Silkworms for Pet Food

You can follow the recommendations for housing laid out in Chapter 3, understanding that if you are raising the worms as pet food, you can be less stringent in your box selections.

Pick a box or boxes that are large enough for the number of worms you hope to produce, and think about your production schedule. You will want to stagger batches of hatching eggs to always have worms on hand for sale or use, as well as allowing some individuals to progress through the entire lifecycle.

Since a single female silk moth can lay hundreds of eggs, your breeding stock can be fairly limited, just make sure you always keep livestock in the various lifecycle stages simultaneously.

The mistake that most people make who try to raise any kind of feeder insect is failure to plan their inventory based on the creature's reproductive cycle.

Silkworms tend to be highly predictable, so with a little initial effort, you should be able to work out a steady supply schedule.

Your worms' growth rates will fall somewhere within these parameters:

- egg to 1 inch / 2.54 cm - 12 days
- 1 inch to 3 inches / 2.54 cm – 7.62 cm - 30 days
- spinning of the cocoons - days 28-30

The pupa will spend about 2 weeks inside the cocoon before the adult moths emerge. They mate, die, and lay their eggs within a few hours, starting the entire process again.

1) *Starter Breeding Kits*

Large scale insect supply houses like Mulberry Farms (www.mulberryfarms.com) make it quite easy for beginners to purchase starter breeding kits. This may be a more economical and efficient way to get started.

The company offers an Economy Starter Package Kit, which it lists as ideal for hobbyists and schools for $200 /£122, with a "large volume" breeder kit selling for $300 /£183.

B) Feeding Silkworms as Pet Food

When you are not concerned about providing your silkworms with the necessary nutrition to produce high-quality silk, their nutritional needs are much more flexible.

In fact, the worms can go for as long as a week without food. You do have to be careful, however, that they don't become dehydrated, so some volume of food once a day is recommended for the moisture content. Silkworms do not drink water.

As a rule, the less you feed the worms, the less they will grow, allowing you to set target sizes according to the needs of your own pets or those of your clientele.

It's fine to use either mulberry leaves or commercial silkworm food. Many people grate the food or break it into small chunks for more even distribution.

Commercial foods come as powders intended to be mixed — but not over mixed — with water. A typical price is $10 /£6.11 per half pound / .23 kg, which will yield 2 lbs. /.9 kg.

These foods are extremely flexible, since they can be stored for up to a year in powdered form and will keep for 2 months in the refrigerator after being mixed with water.

Remember, you have to put the worms directly on the food. They won't go looking for it!

1) Handling the Worms

Always wash your hands before working with the worms or with their food to cut down on the potential for bacterial growth. All containers should be well ventilated.

Maintain temperatures in the room of 78 - 88 F / 26 C – 31C, but do not allow condensation to form in their container. Make sure the food you give the worms is not damp, which can contribute to a buildup of humidity.

Remove waste matter and uneaten, dried-out food from the boxes every day.

When the worms are large enough for the containers to become crowded, transfer them to larger containers, or separate them into smaller batches. Handle the worms with extreme care.

C) Finding a Market for Your Worms

You may have to get creative to find a steady market for your silkworms. Your best bet is to find local customers rather than attempting to deal with live shipping the worms.

Consider contacting local pet stores and negotiating an arrangement to supply them with live silkworms for their customers.

If you are comfortable with having customers come to your home or making deliveries, you can also place advertisements in the newspapers. If you opt to deliver, remember to consider the cost of fuel.

Many online reptile discussion forums allow members to post ads for feeder insects. Do not presume this is the case, however, until you have officially joined the forum and become conversant with its culture and etiquette.

Price according to what the local market will bear. Typically silkworms do cost more than other feeder insects like crickets or mealworms. Online, 30 medium silkworms sell for about $30 /£18.

Obviously unless you have a tremendous volume and a ready market, this is hardly a business in which you will get rich. However, as one sericulturist described her earnings, she does take in "grocery money."

Basically, your hobby can pay for itself, particularly once your production line and breeding stock are both well established.

If you are raising silkworms to feed your own pet reptiles, you'll save yourself a great deal of money, and have an interesting, second hobby.

Don't rule out the possibility of selling cocoons from which your moths have emerged, but unless you're feeding your worms mulberry leaves, the fiber won't be of good enough quality to be of interest to artisans.

Chapter 6) – Common Problems with Silkworms

Although rearing silkworms is, for the most part, a straightforward business, there are problems that can arise. Most of these issues stem from poorly maintained hygiene.

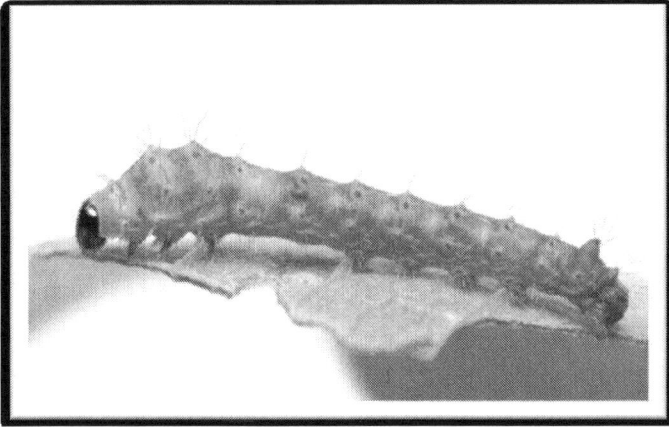

It is absolutely imperative that you wash your hands with soap and dry them on a clean towel before handling your worms or anything that will come into contact with them.

Their containers must be kept clean and free of debris at all times. If cardboard boxes are used, make sure they have not previously housed any substance that would be a contaminant.

The boxes should be completely dry and lined with clean wax paper or paper towels to provide an additional layer of protection for the worms and to facilitate daily maintenance.

Plastic or glass containers should be washed thoroughly with soap and water and dried well before the worms are placed inside. Again, liners should be used.

A) Eggs That Don't Hatch

A number of issues can cause silkworm eggs to fail to hatch. Overheating tops this list. When eggs have gotten too hot, they take on a reddish cast and flatten out.

Another major issue is exposure to water or condensation. In this instance, the eggs will appear to swell, and become a darker blue.

(If the eggs get wet accidentally and are quickly and gently dried by patting with a paper towel, they should still hatch).

It's not only important to ensure good ventilation in your breeding container, but you may find that you have to monitor both temperature and humidity.

Try to maintain approximately 78 F / 26 C and humidity of 80-85%. At lower temperatures, your eggs may be too cold to hatch.

Any time you seek to increase heat in the room where the silkworm eggs are being kept, heat the entire room evenly, don't subject the eggs to direct heat from any kind of lamp. This will easily result in over-heating.

B) Issues with Hatchlings

If your silkworms appear to have shriveled up, they did not get enough to eat, and died of hunger and dehydration. Hatchlings that simply disappear have likely been the victim of marauding ants.

If ants are a problem in the area where you are raising your worms, put the entire container in which the worms are housed in a tray of shallow water. This will keep the ants from being able to reach your livestock.

If your silkworms appear to be in immediate, writhing distress, flip wildly back and forth, and excrete a brownish juice, they have been exposed to insecticide on the mulberry leaves you are using for food.

Generally the symptoms of insecticide poisoning show up within 6-12 hours. You will need to locate a new source of chemical-free mulberry leaves to prevent a recurrence of the poisoning.

C) Common Silkworm Diseases

Although diseases that afflict silkworms vary by location, those that are most common include the following.

1) Flacherie

Bacteria and viruses singularly or in combination cause flacherie, which often appears in instances of high humidity and wide temperature fluctuations, especially if mold builds up on old mulberry leaves and in the accumulated fass or droppings.

The silkworms become very lethargic and do not grow as quickly as they should. Portions of their bodies become translucent and they begin to vomit green to brown liquid and excrete chain-like feces.

A foul odor will permeate the box, and when dead worms are removed, they will break open. This factor alone causes the disease to rapidly spread to healthy worms in the container.

Unfortunately, this disease is almost impossible to eradicate unless the entire colony of worms is destroyed. Take the dead worms and all material from the box and place them in a bag. Put the back in the freezer for several days to kill any microorganisms present.

Discard or wash all containers and fixtures before using them again. The best practice after an outbreak of flacherie is to wait three months before attempting to raise more silkworms.

2) *Grasserie*

Grasserie is caused by a virus and, like flacherie, is also a consequence of poor hygiene and potentially a poor diet.

Again, the worms will begin to be sluggish in their behavior and will seem to swell. Their bodies are easily subject to breaking open, with a milky discharge leaking from the wounds.

As the larva die, they will hang downward from any surface to which they can attach themselves. Worms afflicted with grasserie will not molt and will never be able to spin their cocoons.

The same procedures to dispose of the dead and diseased worms is recommended as described above for flacherie with a similar waiting period before raising more worms.

3) *White and Green Muscardine*

Fungus present on the mulberry leaves is responsible for outbreaks of both white and green muscardine. It is common during the winter months and during periods of high rainfall.

The worms become lethargic and have oily specks on their skin. After death, they become hard and dry, taking on a white or green color and appearing to be almost mummified.

In order to prevent a recurrence, monitor the humidity levels in the growing area more stringently and be extra vigilant about cleaning the cages and maintaining good hygiene.

4) Pebrine

A protozoan that slows the growth of the larvae and causes small blackish brown spots to appear on their skin causes pebrine in silkworms.

This is the disease studied by Louis Pasteur in 1865. Pebrine prevents the worms from spinning their cocoons and is 100% fatal in any infected batch of eggs.

The worms eat the protozoan present on their mulberry leaves in the larval stage and the disease is then passed to the adult moths and into the next generation of eggs.

The only way to stop the process is to inspect the adult moths under a microscope and to cull infected specimens to halt the cycle of the disease.

D) Prevention is the Best Medicine

In all cases, scrupulous hygiene is the best preventive medicine for your silkworms. There are really no "treatments" for any of the conditions that can afflict these delicate creatures. It stands to reason, therefore, that the best option is to head off those diseases before they become established.

When your worms do become infected with any of these conditions, the humane course of action is to destroy the worms by freezing them. Disinfecting all equipment, or discarding the implements and starting over after a 3 month waiting period should ensure that there is no lingering disease in the immediate environment.

Chapter 7) Estimated Set-Up Costs

Please note that the items listed below may vary widely per individual setup. Most sericulturists rapidly develop their own way of doing things. In order to track your costs, I strongly recommend you keep a notebook.

Take down not only the price of your supplies, but also their effectiveness in your silk-raising process. Over the first few months, you will be continuing to refine your technique and deciding what works best for you.

A) Silkworm Eggs

Silkworm eggs are typically shipped halfway through their incubation period, and will hatch within a week of arrival. There are multiple purchase options.

1) Lots in Multiples of 100

Most supply houses will offer lots of silkworm eggs in multiples of 100 glued down in a petri dish. Typical pricing for this type of packaging ranges from 200-1000 eggs for $9.50-$21 / £5.80-£13.

2) Loose Eggs in Bulk

Purchasing loose eggs in bulk can be considerably cheaper, with 2000 eggs selling for $20 / £12.

If you buy loose eggs in bulk, however, you will need to purchase additional petri dishes to ensure that the eggs are not overcrowded for hatching. Expect to pay approximately $7-$10 / £4-£6 for medium to large petri dishes in packs of 20.

3) Shipped with Ice Packs

Most suppliers add an additional charge for shipping the eggs overnight with ice-packs. It is not unusual for this provision to be offered for bulk orders of several thousands only. Expect an additional cost of $5-$10 / £3-£6 per shipment for the special packaging. Postage will vary by region and distance.

B) Live Silkworms

Especially if you are raising silkworms for feeder insects, you may want to begin your process with a batch of live silkworms. Pricing is typically according to size, with lots offered in multiples of 100 for smaller worms (.5 inch / 1.27 cm or less) and multiples of 25 for larger specimens (.75-1 inch / 1.9-2.54 cm).

Small worms cost approximately $8 / £5 per lot of 100, with medium worms available for approximately $7 / £4 for lots of 25.

C) Silkworm Starter Package

Many people who decide to raise silkworms as feeder insects find it far easier to begin with a silkworm starter package from a company like Mulberry Farms (www.mulberryfarms.com). These kits are also ideal for silkworm projects in the classroom.

small kit $200 / £122
large kit $300 / £183

D) Dried Silkworm Food

Powdered foods retail for approximately $11 / £7 per 0.5 pound / 0.22 kg, but may be less expensive if bought in larger quantities. Typically 0.5 pounds / 0.22 kg of dried food will yield 2 lbs. / 0.9 kg of prepared food.

(Note, that if you do not have access to fresh mulberry leaves, dried food is a potentially ongoing expense and should be figured into your long-term cost calculations).

E) Mulberry Leaves

While it may be possible to buy mulberry leaves from various sources, bear in mind that the leaves are the silkworm's only supply of moisture. The worms will die if they become dehydrated, so dried out leaves will do them no good.

Such products, when offered, are generally priced at around \$4 / £2.50 for roughly half a pound (200-250 grams.)

Exercise caution, however, as the "shelf" life of mulberry leaves is quite short. You would do better to find a local and readily available source for mulberry leaves.

F) Mulberry Trees

If you live in a region where a white mulberry tree will grow, and you decide to go this route not only to augment your sericulture project, but perhaps to enhance your landscaping, a 5-6 foot / 1.52-1.8 meter white mulberry tree from a nursery will cost approximately \$50 / £30.

(Please note that this price does not include potential ancillary expenses like delivery and planting of the tree itself).

G) Rearing Supplies

Freezer or wax paper to serve as box liners
\$1.50-\$2.00 / £0.91-£1.22 per roll

A series of successive plastic boxes with vented lids. (Please note that all prices and suggested measurements are approximations).

6" x 6" / 15.24cm x 15.24 cm
\$1.75-\$2.50 / £1.68-£1.52

12" x 24" / 31cm x 61cm
$12-$14 / £7.32-£8.54

Note that simple cardboard boxes can be used if they are clean and free of contaminants. Spinning containers can be made of old egg cartons, or cut sections of toilet tissue or paper towel rolls.

If you purchase new cardboard boxes, expect to buy in lots of 12-25. As an example, 25 cardboard boxes with dimensions of 6" x 6" x 6" (15.24cm x 15.24cm x 15.24cm) would cost approximately $10 / £6.

Thermometer with hygrometer:
Digital unit $15-$25 / £9-£15
Analog unit $10-$12 / £6-£7

H) Reeling Supplies

Multiple boilers /sauce pans and a slow cooker

3 quart / 2.8 liter sauce pan
$10-$20 / £6-£12

Slow cooker, 1.5 quart / 1.4 liter
$12-$15 / £7.3-£9

Slotted spoons
$5 / £3 each

Round dish brush

$5 / £3

Clock reel yarn winder
$250 / £153+

Please note that the above prices will vary widely. Many sericulture enthusiasts make their own reeling devices or commission custom devices from craftsmen.

I) Degumming Supplies

Colander
$5-$15 / £3-£9

Washing soda
55 ounces / 1.5 kg
$9 / £5

Vinegar
64 ounces / 1.89 liters
$3 / £1.8

J) Mawatas Supplies

If you plan to stretch your cocoons by hand into mawatas or hankies, you will need the sort of stretcher frame typically used by needlepoint and cross stitch artisans. Simply place nails, thumbtacks, or pegs in the corners to secure your square of silk.

A sturdy, reusable stretcher frame in the 6" x 6" / 15.24cm x 15.24 cm range will cost approximately $20 / £12.

A drop spindle is a good and simple method for spinning yarn from mawatas. Depending on size and materials, a spindle will cost from $15-$25 / £9-£15.

K) Ancillary Supplies

As indicated in the text, it's almost impossible to guess where any one person will go with an individual sericulture endeavor. You may well decide, after successfully reeling silk from cocoons for the first time, that you are now interested in spinning thread or yarn.

Spinning almost inevitably leads to dying, which may, in turn, lead to a new interest in weaving. At the very least, you're likely to purchase books along the way to investigate these options.

My best advice to you in this regard is to go not just where you can see a chance for profit, but where the sericulture hobby leads you in terms of creativity and joy.

Allow sericulture to become what is best for you in your individual circumstances and enjoy the ride!

L) Investment in Time

Although I have emphasized this point before, I feel it necessary, in keeping with the notion that time is money, to say it again — make sure you can invest the necessary time to take care of your silkworms before you take up home sericulture!

The worms must be supplied with a constant source of food. Their diet provides both nourishment and moisture. At the height of their growth rate, the worms eat 24 hours a day.

While the investment required to get started in sericulture may be minimal, like any project, you will begin to develop a degree of emotional attachment to the success of the endeavor. It can be truly heartbreaking to lose all your worms due to poor hygiene in their environment or inadequate feeding.

This means you will also need to think of the welfare of your worms in the event that you must be away from them. If you do not have someone who understands how to care for the silkworms in your absence, especially during a vacation, it would be best to plan your production schedule around your trip and not have any worms hatching, feeding, or spinning while you are gone.

Given the rapid growth rate of newly hatched silkworms, it won't be difficult for you to be back up to operating speed after an absence, and such an interruption can be a perfect opportunity to thoroughly clean or completely change out all your rearing boxes and associated equipment for fresh items.

Afterword

In truth, the process of raising silkworms has changed very little over thousands of years. It is a business that involves hard work and delicate care.

For their lifespan, the silkworms can be demanding little taskmasters, eating constantly and growing rapidly in preparation for the task of spinning their gossamer thread.

There is something marvelous about the notion that those cocoons are comprised of a single strand of pure, raw silk. When unraveled, that silk can be spun into glistening thread, dyed, and then woven into prized luxury fabric.

Although it seems something of a shame to contemplate it, these same industrious worms can also be raised for their nutritional value as pet food. Because silkworms go through four successive molts, they are almost designer reptile food.

When used as feeder insects, silkworms can be raised to scale. They do not bite, and thus are appropriate food for any number of companion reptiles.

There are many reasons for contemplating raising silkworms at home. Some people do it for the pure interest value of watching the world's oldest domesticated insect at work.

In truth, the greatest chance of turning a small profit lies in the feeder insect route, although many artisans raise silkworms in order to produce the fiber they will use in their creations.

By doing so, they are totally in charge of the quality of their product from start to finish. The items are completely unique and can command a high price in the right market. Whether this constitutes a profit, however, is questionable.

The expense of getting started with raising silkworms is small, so a "trial run" is hardly out of the question. This is why silkworms are often popular as classroom projects.

Regardless of your reasons for familiarizing yourself with *Bombyx mori,* you will come away from the experience with a new appreciation for the potential relationship between man and insect.

In recent months it has been suggested by the United Nations that we superior humans under regard insects. These creatures hold the potential not only to provide sources of high nutrition for human beings, but also to serve us in a variety of ways from pest control to waste disposal.

In such a potential service relationship, *Bombyx mori* is the great-great-grandfather of domesticated insects. They have lived in partnership with man for so long, they can no longer survive in the wild.

It would be a disservice to these remarkable creatures, however, to suggest that silkworms are all about the work. If you have never watched one spin its cocoon, you cannot yet appreciate the magic that is part of this process.

Although waggishly referred to as "worm spit" by enthusiasts, silk remains the great luxury fabric of the world, and one that is completely natural. If you decide to become part of the world of sericulture, you are joining a centuries old tradition.

If you have read this far and decided that raising silkworms is not for you, perhaps you will at least go away with a new awareness of and respect for *Bombyx mori.*

The results of his labor opened new avenues of communication between East and West in the days when the Silk Road was the world's longest highway. Though small of body, he has been mighty of endeavor and now, millennia later, his relationship with man continues to thrive.

Relevant Websites

The following websites are offered for informational purposes and were extant at the time of this writing. Since the web is ever changing, I cannot guarantee that any of these resources will remain in place.

Silkworm Information

The Fruitfly Shop
www.buyfruitflies.com/silkworm_info2.html

Guide to Raising Silkworms
www.silkwormstore.co.uk/guide-to-raising-silkworms.html

The History of Sericulture
www.silkroadcreations.com/history-of-sericulture.html

Worm Spit
www.wormspit.com

Blogs

Caterpillars and Cocoons
www.caterpillarsandcocoons.blogspot.com/

The Silkworms Take Halifax
www.thesilkwormstakehalifax.wordpress.com

Worm Spit Blog
www.wormspit.com/blog

Educational Uses

Sue Kayton Silkworm Information
www.suekayton.com

Communities and Discussion Groups

Silk Reelers (Yahoo Group)
www.groups.yahoo.com/group/silkreelers/join

Cat Herders (Yahoo Group)
www.groups.yahoo.com/group/CatHerders/join

Videos

How to Use Silk Hankies
www.youtube.com/watch?v=lDbdmn8yCB8

The Life Cycle of the Silkworm
www.youtube.com/watch?v=J8A2sn4Uzfo

Mechanization in Sericulture
www.youtube.com/watch?v=0kgZWPFnM3o

MIT Media
www.creativeapplications.net/environment

Reeling Silk
www.youtube.com/watch?v=vbDuIP2Q2lQ

Silk Factory
www.youtube.com/watch?v=BibC0CqZhPI

Silk Farm in Cambodia
www.youtube.com/watch?v=QLb-tM0Xi4g

Silkworms Making Cocoons
www.youtube.com/watch?v=HwP827yRIxs

Silkworms – Time Lapse
www.youtube.com/watch?v=UtHjDRVRM_Y

Spinning Silk
www.youtube.com/watch?v=2Kr84EFmWcY

Spinning Silk Hankies
www.youtube.com/watch?v=tZtZ90iqja8

Stretching Silk Cocoons
www.youtube.com/watch?v=P_OpFgQ4HTk

Where to Buy Silkworms - US

Aurora Silk
www.aurorasilk.com/

Carolina Pet Supply
http://www.carolinapetsupply.com/

InsectNet
www.insectnet.com/

Lady Silkworm
www.ladysilkworm.com/

Mulberry Farms
www.mulberryfarms.com/

Silkworm Shop
www.silkwormshop.com/index.html

Treenway Silks
www.treenwaysilks.com/

The Yarn Tree
www.theyarntree.com/

Where to Buy Silkworms - UK

www.silkwormstore.co.uk

www.wwb.co.uk/silkworm-eggs-colourful-cocoons-and-unusual-larvae

www.joannarosetidey.com/bombyx-mori-silk-worms/school-silkworm-kits-uk-2/

www.rickslivefood.co.uk/vmchk/Silkworm-Eggs/View-all-products.html

www.butterworms.co.uk/24-500-silkworm-eggs.html

Where to Buy Silkworms – Australia

Everything Silkworms
www.everythingsilkworms.com.au/

Peaceful Silkworms
www.peacefulsilkworms.com.au

Frequently Asked Questions

Typically I might caution my readers to read the text carefully and then delve into the frequently asked questions, but in truth, you will discover that the longer you read about the world of raising silkworms, the more there is to learn.

I encourage you to seek out all sources of information to sharpen your knowledge of the relationship between man and this industrious little insect. If you are the sort of reader who enjoys getting a quick "jump" on the text, this is the section for you!

Where does silk come from?

If you are referring to the fiber itself, silk comes straight from the worm's mouth. The strand is essentially worm "spit" — one long, continuous strand of it.

If you mean where did the practice of raising silkworms to cultivate the fiber originate, the answer is China.

Is it hard to raise silkworms?

In terms of difficulty, no, but the process does require great care, an absolutely clean environment, and a steady supply of mulberry leaves.

How does silk compare to other materials on the market?

Silk is superior in strength to all other plant and animal fibers, even though it's lightweight and somewhat delicate in appearance. The fabric is cool in the summer, yet comfortable in the colder months.

Although resistant to heat and fairly elastic, silk will yellow in direct sunlight and it is weakened by perspiration, perfumes, deodorants, and other chemicals.

Are certain parts of the world specifically associated with the silk industry?

Raw silk comes primarily from China, but India, and Japan are also major leaders in the industry. France is famous for its production of finished silk fabrics.

What exactly is a silkworm?

The silkworm is actually the larval stage of the silk moth, an insect domesticated into the service of man for many thousands of years.

After I receive silkworm eggs in the mail, how long will it be before they hatch?

Typically, silkworm eggs shipped via mail hatch within a week of arrival if they are kept at a temperature between 78-85 F / 26-29 C.

Is there anything I need to do to help the eggs to hatch?

Keeping the eggs at a temperature between 78-85 F / 26-29 C is all that is required to allow your silkworm eggs to hatch.

Are the eggs I order guaranteed to hatch?

You will have to refer to the guarantee policies of the entity from which you ordered the eggs, but in most cases 90-95% of eggs in a shipped batch will hatch.

Obviously the more eggs you order, the greater the hatched number, but always remember that raising silkworms is a matter of scale. Unless you can care for 500 worms, don't order 500 eggs. (They won't all hatch, but you get my point).

It is critical that the worms not be over crowded, so make sure you have enough room for the larva at each stage of their development.

Supply houses typically sell silkworm eggs in lots of 200, 500, and 1000. Most arrive in petri dishes. If it's an option to do so, request that the eggs be placed in extra-large dishes to ensure adequate space for optimum hatching.

Can I delay the hatching of the eggs if I place them in the refrigerator?

You will need to refer to the shipping policies and methods of the supply house with which you are working.

If you have received the eggs via overnight shipment and they arrive packed with an ice pack, you can place them in a refrigerator at 35-37 F / 1.6-2.7 C at 70-80% humidity for as long as a month.

When removed from the refrigerator, the eggs should hatch in 8-10 days if kept at approximately 78-80 F / 26-27 C.

Should I count the eggs to make sure I received a full order?

In my experience, even if you think a petri dish of eggs does not have as many eggs as you ordered, in reality there will likely be more eggs than the specified amount, not fewer. If I were you, I seriously would not attempt to count all those tiny little eggs. It's wasted effort!

What should I feed my silkworms?

Under ideal circumstances, silkworms eat mulberry leaves, although they can be fed a powdered artificial diet. The latter, however, may not be ideal for optimum production of silk fiber. Frankly, opinions vary on this point.

105

Please refer to Chapter 3 - The Basics of Sericulture for more information on diet.

If I run out of mulberry leaves, is there anything else I can feed my silkworms?

In an emergency, you can feed your silkworms washed, raw, unpeeled, grated carrots for a few days, but you must get them back on mulberry leaves as quickly as possible. (Don't be alarmed if the worms turn a little orange).

Should I use a substrate in my breeding and rearing boxes?

There is no need to add a substrate to the boxes, but a lining of wax paper or paper towels will help to facilitate cleaning.

How fast will my silkworms mature?

If maintained at a temperature of approximately 85 F / 29 C and given all they can eat, the worms should reach a size of 1 inch / 2.54 cm in about two weeks, 2 inches / 5.08 cm in 3 weeks, and 3 inches / 7.62 cm in a month.

What is the absolutely ideal temperature?

If you stay in a range of 78-85 F / 26-29 C your silkworms should thrive.

I'm going to use prepared food. I bought 1 pound / 0.45 kg. How many worms will that feed?

A single pound / 0.45 kg is enough to feed 20-25 silkworms throughout their entire lifecycle. If, however, you are raising the worms as feeder insects, a pound will feed 1000 silkworms until they reach a length of 1.5 inches / 3.81 cm.

How long can artificial foods be stored?

Estimates vary by brand, but most companies indicate that their preparations in powdered form can be stored for as long as 6 months to a year. Once the food is mixed with water, it's generally good for a few weeks in the refrigerator.

How do worms that are used to one food react to another?

Worms that have been receiving artificial food will attack mulberry leaves with enthusiasm. If, however, the worms have been getting leaves and are switched to artificial food, you may have to apply the mixture to green lettuce leaves to entice them to eat.

How does the food used affect the worms' ability to spin cocoons?

This is actually a matter of some debate. Some sericulturists say that the worms will spin cocoons on an artificial diet, but that the silk will be of lesser quality. Others insist that the worms will not spin at all unless they are given mulberry leaves.

Is it possible to identify the gender of a silk moth visually?

Female silk moths are about 2 cm larger than males and have larger abdomens.

Can silk moths fly?

No, silk moths cannot fly, nor do they having working mouth parts.

How long do the adult moths live?

The moths mate within 12-24 hours of emerging from the cocoon. The males die first, and the females die after laying their eggs.

Glossary

Bombyx mori - The Latin name for the silkworm or larval stage of a moth in the *Bombicidae* family that is most commonly used in silk production. The worms, or caterpillars, which feed on the leaves of mulberry trees, spin cocoons of pure, white silk, which, when unwound, are turned into silk thread.

Cocoon - The silk moth larva or caterpillar, commonly known as the silkworm, spins an oval casing, cocoon or chrysalis, to protect itself during the pupa stage of development. The single filament, which is white to golden yellow in color, is unwound to produce raw silk fiber.

Gegumming - The term to describe the process whereby the natural gum, or sericin, that binds the fibers of the silkworm's cocoon together is removed to allow for the production of silk thread.

Fibroin - Eighty percent of raw silk fiber is comprised of this protein, which is transformed from the protein present in the mulberry leaves silkworms consume during their larval stage.

Filament - The term used to describe the single strand of silk in a silkworm's cocoon that can be 984-3937 feet / 300-1200 meters in length.

Hankie - Also known as a Mawata Square, a hankie is a partially degummed square of silk that has been expanded by hand and stretched over a frame to a dimension of roughly 10 x 10 inches / 25.4 x 25.4 cm.

Larva - The singular of the word larvae, referring to the juvenile form of the silkworm moth, which undergoes four progressive molts before spinning a cocoon to evolve from a pupae into an adult moth.

Molting - The process by which the silkworm moth sheds its skin in order to become largest. The worms or caterpillars go through four successive molds to reach an eventual length of 3 inches / 7.62 cm before spinning their cocoons.

Mulberry - The common name for *Morus alba*, a tree that is the sole food for *Bombyx mori*, the larval form of the silkworm moth responsible for spinning silk fiber into cocoons, which are then unreeled to make silk thread.

Pupa - The life stage of the silkworm in the cocoon prior to metamorphosis when the creature emerges as the silk moth. Typically, the pupa are killed in the cocoons by submersion in boiling water so that the silk fiber may be harvested intact.

Raw silk - Raw silk is the continuous length of unbroken silk fiber still covered in sericin that is unreeled from the cocoons spun by silkworms to protect them during the pupa stage.

Sericin - Also known as "silk gum," this sticky protein serves to coat the filaments of a silkworm's cocoon and bind them together. It is typically removed before raw silk is spun into thread.

Sericulture - The practice of cultivating silkworms for the purpose of extracting raw silk from their cocoons.

Silk Road - Also known as the Silk Route, this is the name given to the 4,000 mile trade route that connected China to Asia Minor and the Mediterranean and served to connect the civilizations of the East and West, helping to lay the foundations of the modern world. Began during the Han Dynasty (206 BC – 220 AD.)

Index

Published by IMB Publishing 2015

Printed in Great Britain
by Amazon